IS THERE LIFE AFTER 60?

by TONI GOFFE

First published in Great Britain by
Pendulum Gallery Press
56 Ackender Road, Alton, Hants GU34 1JS

© TONI GOFFE 1993

IS THERE LIFE AFTER 60?
ISBN 0-948912-24-3

HELP!! I'M SIXTY!!

PRINTED IN GREAT BRITAIN BY
UNWIN BROTHERS LTD, OLD WOKING, SURREY

I SHOULD HAVE KNOWN HE WASN'T UP TO BLOWING OUT ALL THOSE CANDLES AT HIS AGE...

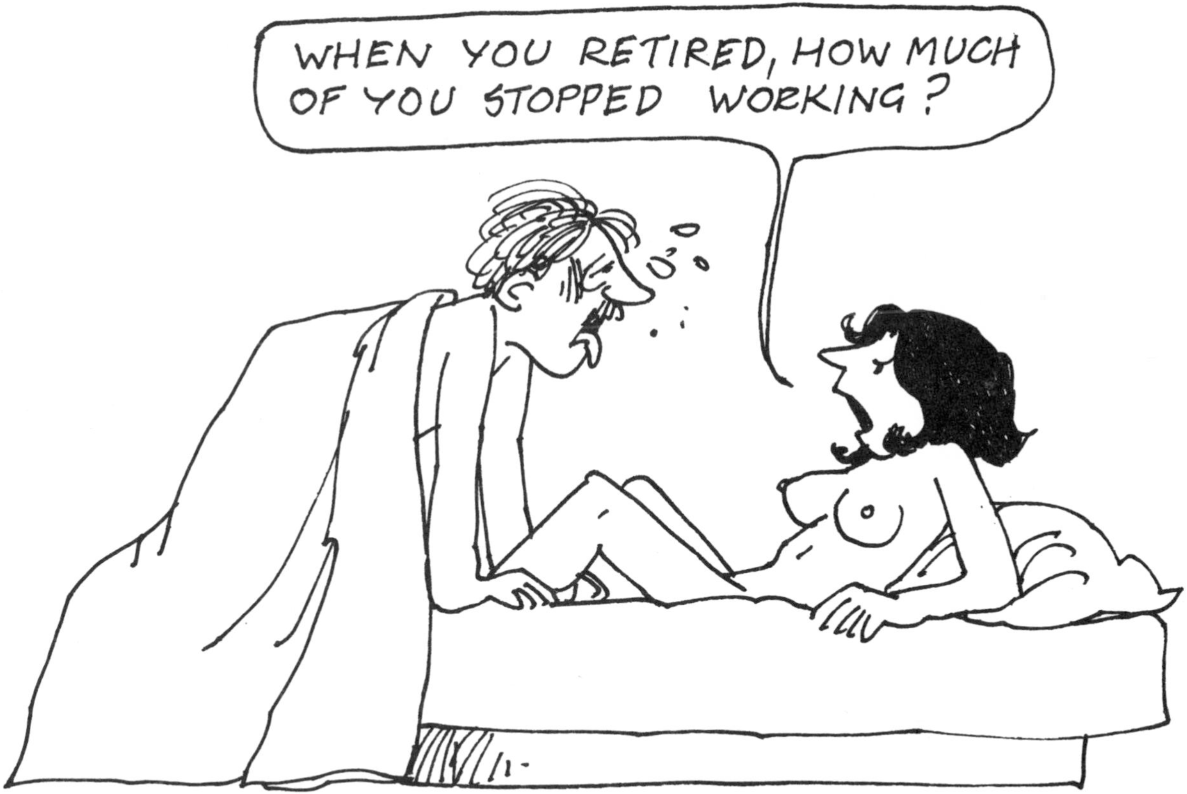
WHEN YOU RETIRED, HOW MUCH OF YOU STOPPED WORKING?

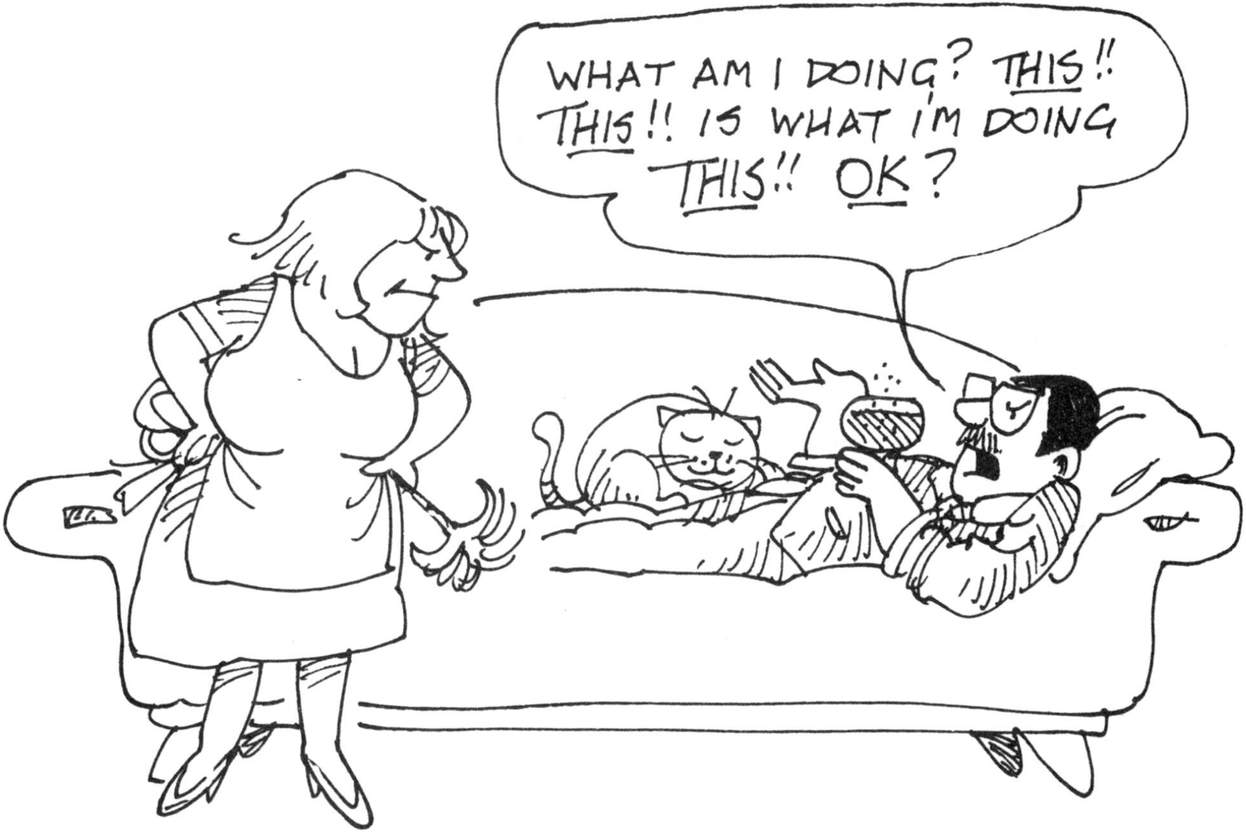
WHAT AM I DOING? THIS!! THIS!! IS WHAT I'M DOING THIS!! OK?

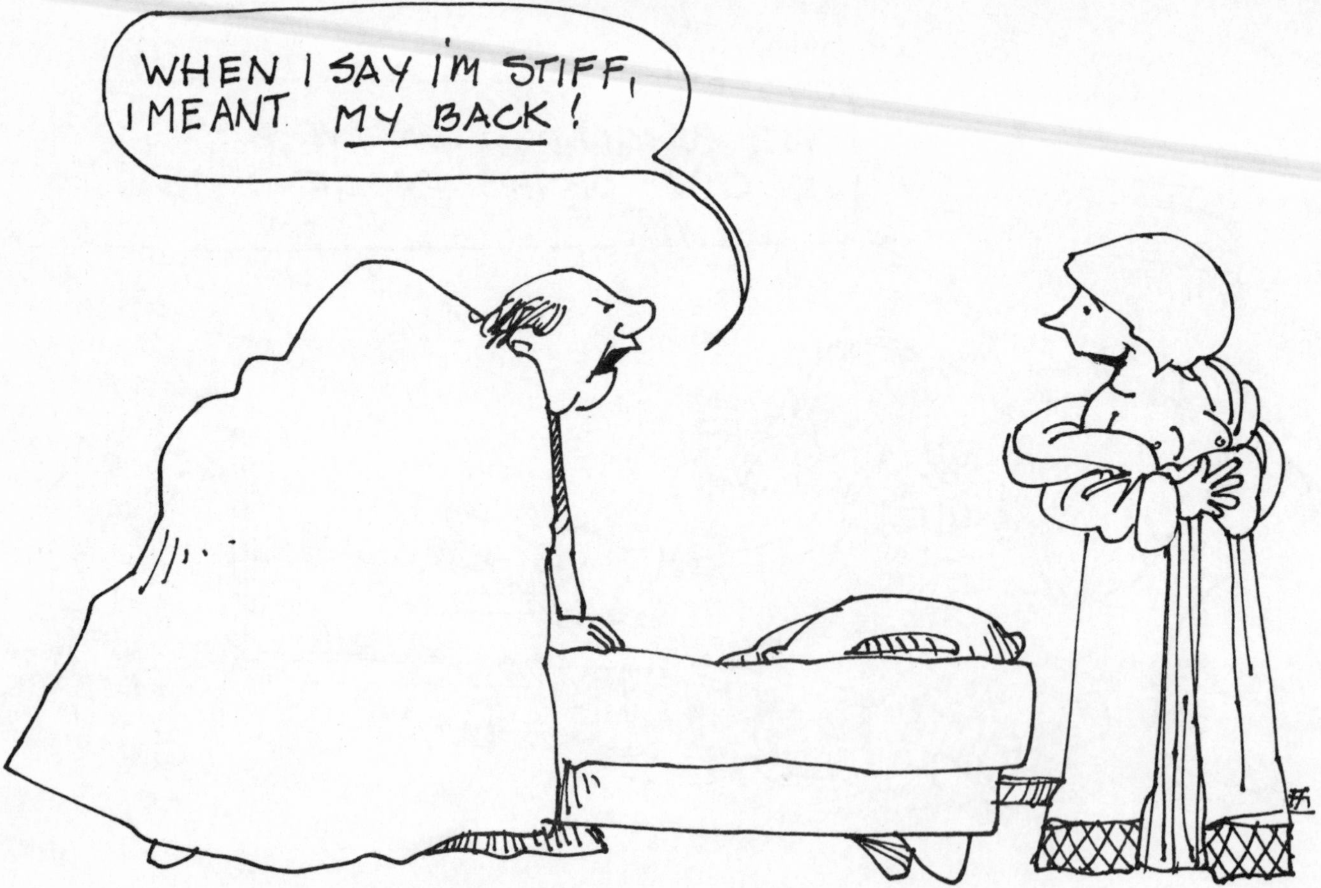
WHEN I SAY I'M STIFF, I MEANT MY BACK!

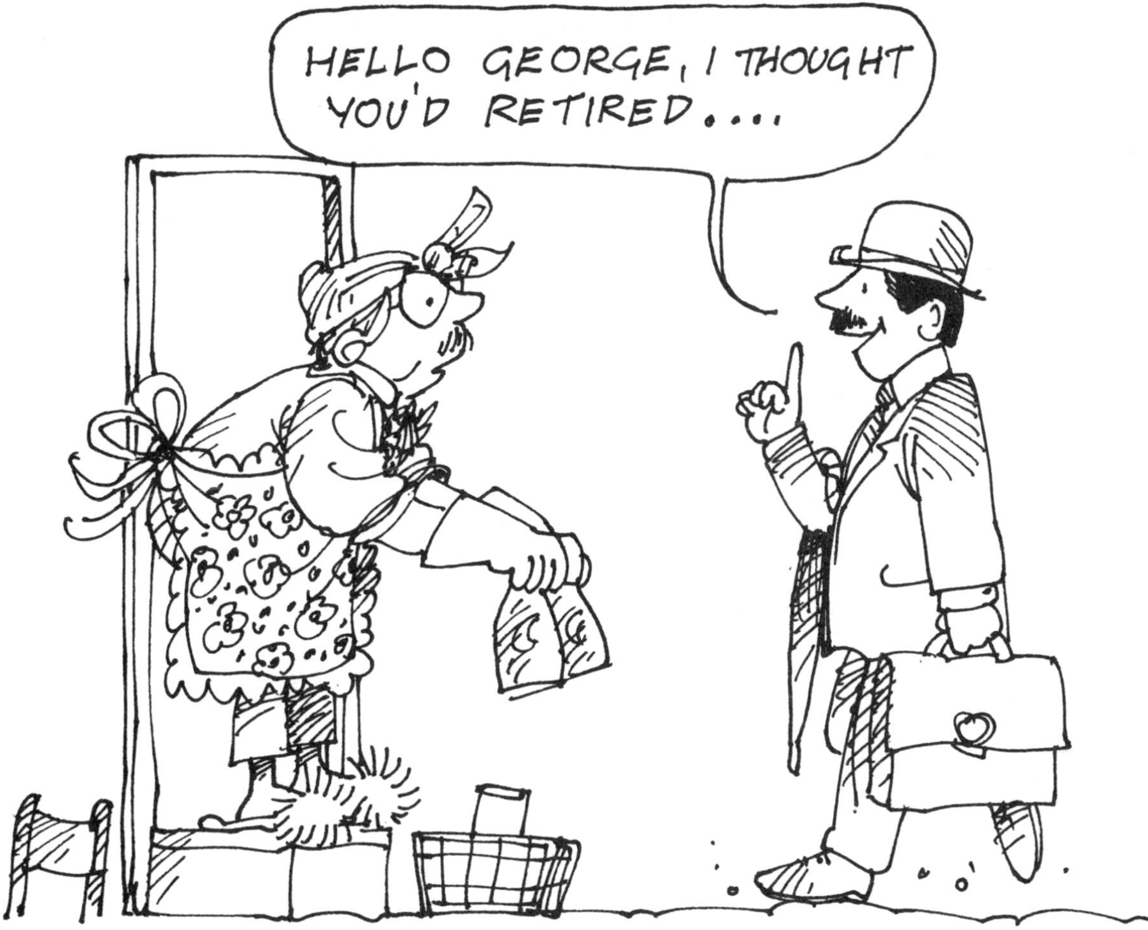
HELLO GEORGE, I THOUGHT YOU'D RETIRED....

WE SEEM TO READ A LOT MORE BOOKS NOW, THAN WE DID WHEN WE WERE YOUNGER DON'T WE ?

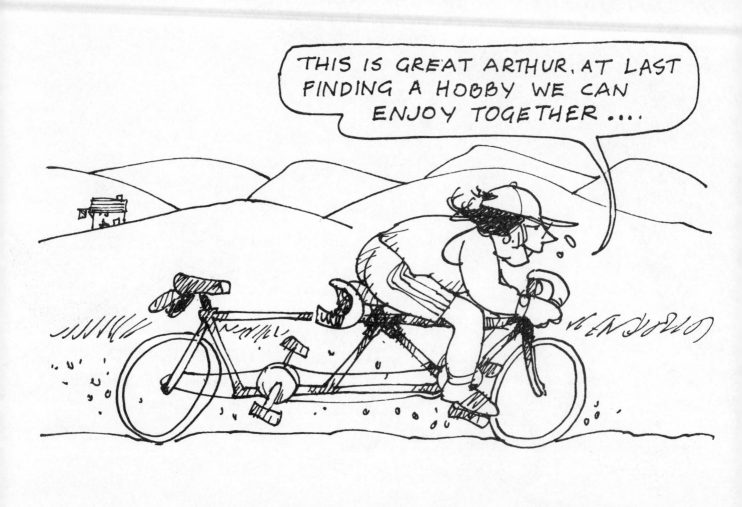

ALICE! IT'S MY TURN TO PICK OUR
HOLIDAY VENUE NEXT YEAR — RIGHT!?

I SAID! IF YOU'RE EYESIGHT IS THAT BAD YOU SHOULD GET YOUR EARS TESTED SO YOU CAN HEAR WHAT THE OPTICIAN IS GOING TO SAY.....

I THINK I'LL PLANT OUT SOME PEAS FOR NEXT
YEAR WHEN I GET BACK TO THE ALLOTMENT....